EUDIST PRAYERBOOK SERIES:
VOLUME 3

# A HOLY WEEK EVERY WEEK

## WEEKDAY MEDITATIONS
### by St. John Eudes

Compiled by *Heart of Home* from:
**The Life And The Kingdom Of Jesus in Christian Souls: A Treatise On Christian Perfection For Use By Clergy Or Laity**

Translated from the French
by Thomas Merton.
Originally published 1946
(New York: P. J. Kenedy & Sons)

**Cover image:** a 40 ton marble statue of St. John Eudes in St. Peter's Basilica. Carved in 1932 by Silvio Silva, this is one of 39 large statues around the Basilica's nave and transepts honoring the founders of great religious orders.

ISBN: 978-0-9979114-2-8

Copyright ©2018, by
The Eudists – Congregation of Jesus and Mary, US Region

Published by

744 Sonrisa Street
Solana Beach, CA 92075
www.eudistsusa.org

# Table of Contents

# Preface

St. Paul reminds us that we should pray without ceasing
(1 Thessalonians 5:16-18).

St. John Eudes also speaks to us of the necessity of prayer:
*"The holy exercise of prayer must be considered one of the chief foundations
of Christian life and sanctity, since the whole life of Jesus Christ was nothing
but a perpetual prayer, which you must continue and express in your life.
This is so necessary that the earth on which you live, the air you breathe, the
bread that sustains you, the heart that beats in your breast, none of them are so
necessary to man for his bodily life as prayer is to a Christian if he is to live as
a Christian."* (*The Life And The Kingdom Of Jesus*: Part 1, Chapter 2,
Section VIII)

A short time later he continues:
*"Prayer is perfect delight, supreme happiness, a true earthly paradise. It is by
this divine exercise of prayer that the Christian soul is united to God, who is
the center of its being, its goal and its supreme good. It is in prayer that God
belongs to the soul and the soul to God. It is by praying that the soul pays Him
rightful service, homage, adoration and love, and receives from Him His lights,
His blessings and a thousand tokens of His exceeding great love. It is during
your prayers that God takes His delight in you, according to this word of His:*

"My delights are to be with the children of men" (Prov. 8:31)

*This gives us a tangible expression of the fact that our true joy and perfect
satisfaction are to be found in God, and that a hundred, or even a thousand
years of the false pleasures of this world are not worth one moment of the true
delights which God allows those souls to taste, who seek all their contentment
only in conversing with Him in holy prayer."*

Finally, Fr. Eudes shows us a way to spend each day of the week
meditating on the life of Christ:
*"In order to spend the days of your week devoutly, it is a good thing to dedicate
each day to some mystery of the life of Christ, in order to give particular honor
to His life on that day and to try to implant its special virtues in your soul by
consideration and imitation.*

1

*According to St. Paul, we are all dead in Adam and living in Jesus Christ (I Cor. 15:22), and since Jesus Christ is our life (Col. 3:4), none of us have any right to live on earth except by the life of Jesus Christ. Remember that God lets you remain here only so that you may work to destroy in you the wicked and sinful life of the old Adam and to establish within yourself the holy and divine life of Jesus.*

*Hence, your chief care and occupation should be to consider, adore, and imitate the life of Jesus, in order that, by this means, you may form and establish within yourself a perfect image of that life.*

*Here are a few meditations for each day of the week, which sum up the whole life of Jesus, and which I present in the form of prayers, so that every type of person may use them to honor the various phases of the life of Christ."* (*The Life And The Kingdom Of Jesus*: Part 4, Chapter 1, Section II)

This little volume gives St. John Eudes' way to dedicate each day of the week to prayer. Each meditation takes but a few minutes to read. Take a few more minutes to reflect on the mystery.

If you choose to make these meditations part of your morning routine as you prepare for your day, you can bring to mind the mystery he presents throughout your day.

Perhaps you choose to reflect on these at midday. In this way, you can build an island of prayer, and allow the waves from that island to wash over you as you anticipate your meditation, and then as you return to your accustomed activities.

In the evening these meditations can accompany you as you fall asleep, with the thoughts initiated by the particular meditation. Perhaps if you choose an evening routine, you might consider looking ahead to the following day's theme.

We live in a time when our lives are so full — so busy — that we often forget that we are called to constant prayer, as the Saints remind us above. Take time each day to wrap your mind around these themes. As time goes on, the rhythm of the meditations will become a worthwhile habit which can help to sanctify the whole of your life.

Maryann Marshall
Editor, Heart of Home
Lawrenceville, Georgia, 2016

# Sunday

## *The Divine Life of Jesus in the Bosom of His Father from all Eternity*

Oh Jesus, my Lord and my God, I contemplate, adore and glorify You in Your divine life from all eternity in the bosom of the Eternal Father, before Your Incarnation in the virginal womb of Your Mother.

Oh, how holy a life it is: how pure, divine, wonderful and filled with glory, greatness and delights! What joy to see You living, from all eternity, a life so filled with perfection, contentment and wonders!

Blessed are You, oh Father of Jesus, for having imparted such a life to Your well-beloved Son!

Oh Jesus, I offer You all the glory, love and praise You deserve from the Father and the Holy Spirit throughout the eternity of Your divine life.

Oh Jesus, when I consider Your divine and eternal life, I see that Your chief function for all eternity is to contemplate, glorify and love Your Father, to refer Yourself to Him as to Your principal, to give Him Your being, Your life, Your perfections and all that You shall be forever, as gifts received form Him, to be employed in glorifying and loving Him, and to offer Him infinitely worthy praise and love.

Blessed are You, oh Jesus, for all these things.

Oh most lovable Father, how I rejoice to behold You so loved and glorified by Your Son!

I offer You all love and glory that You received from Him during all eternity, by His divine life in Your fatherly bosom before His Incarnation.

Oh good Jesus, You have expended all Your divine life for my benefit. From all eternity You think of me, love me and offer me to the Father, and You offer Yourself to Him as well, to come one day upon earth to be made flesh, to suffer and die on earth for love of me.

Oh dearest Jesus, You have loved me from all eternity, and I hardly know if I have yet begun to love You as I should. Forgive me, my Savior. From now on, and for all eternity, let me live for nothing but to love You!

3

# Monday

## *The First Moment of the Temporal Life of Jesus*

Oh Jesus, I adore You at the moment of Your Incarnation, which is the first instant of Your mortal life. I adore all the marvelous things that took place in You at that moment. What great accomplishments were effected in You and by You, in that blessed instant, in the eyes of the Father, the Holy Spirit, Your sacred humanity, and Your Blessed Mother! What thoughts, what affections, what love! How Your holy soul in that instant devoted itself, before Your Father's face, to adore and glorify Him and sacrifice Yourself entirely to His glory, and to accomplish all that He willed!

Oh good Jesus, I adore Your first thoughts and Your first acts of adoration, oblation, love and praise, which You offered to Your Father at that time. How exalted and divine were the love and glory that You gave Him then! Truly You gave Him infinitely more honor and love in that moment alone than all the angels and all men accorded Him in the five thousand years that preceded Your Incarnation, or ever shall give Him for all eternity.

Oh Father of Jesus, what satisfaction for my soul to behold You so loved and glorified by Your Son!

Oh Jesus, be blessed, adored and glorified for ever for the honor and love You gave to Your Father at the blessed moment of Your Incarnation.

Oh Jesus, when I consider You in this mystery, I see by the light of faith that You entertain the most exalted thoughts and great designs for her in whom the Incarnation was accomplished, and that You indeed effect great and marvelous things in her.

Oh Jesus, I adore Your first thoughts, Your first acts of love and movements of grace, of light and of eminent sanctity which You produced in Your Blessed Mother at the moment of Your Incarnation.

So too, I adore the first acts of adoration, praise and love of the most admirable Mother for the most adorable Son.

Blessed are You, oh Jesus, Son of Mary, for all the wonders You worked in Your divine Mother by this stupendous mystery.

Blessed are you, oh Mother of Jesus, for all the glory you have given your Son in this same mystery. Unite me, I implore you, to all the love and honor you gave your Dear Son in the first instant of his life, and grant that I may share in your peerless love for Him and in your zeal for His glory.

Oh most lovable Jesus, at the same instant that You looked up to the Father, after the Incarnation, You also looked upon me. You began to think of Him, refer Yourself to Him and love Him and You likewise began to think of me, to give Yourself to me, and love me. At the very instant You began to live, it was to live for me, to prepare and acquire for me most extraordinary graces, and to form plans for my salvation.

From that very moment You planned and desired to create in me an image of the mystery of Your Incarnation and to become incarnate in me, that is, to unite me to Yourself, and Yourself most intimately to me, both physically and spiritually by Your holy grace and your divine sacraments, and then to fill me with Yourself, and establish Yourself in me to live and reign perfectly in me.

Oh what goodness! What boundless love! Infinitely blessed are You, oh good Jesus! May all Your mercies and all Your wonders for the children of men bless You forever!

I most humbly beg Your forgiveness for the obstacles which I have put in the way of the accomplishment of the great designs You have for me. Never allow me to impede Your grace again. From now on I desire to annihilate, at all costs, everything in me that opposes Your holy will.

My Jesus, may it please You to grant me the grace and strength to do this.

5

# Tuesday

## *The Holy Childhood of Jesus*

Oh great and admirable Jesus, You were not satisfied to become man for love of men, but You also willed to become a child, subject to all the lowliness and weakness of infancy, in order to honor the Eternal Father in every condition of human life, and to sanctify all the states of our life.

Blessed are You, good Jesus, for these favors. May all Your angels and saints bless You eternally.

Oh most lovable Child, I offer You my own childhood, although it is past, imploring You most humbly that, by virtue of Your divine Childhood, You may wipe out all that was bad or imperfect and cause my whole life as a child to render homage to Your most adorable Childhood.

Oh divine Jesus, when I contemplate You in Your holy Childhood, I see that You are never idle, but effect great things for Your Eternal Father, contemplating, adoring and loving Him, and also for Your Blessed Mother, heaping upon her a world of graces and blessings, also for St. Joseph, and little St. John the Baptist and the other saints with whom You associated as a child, accomplishing in them most wonderful works of illumination and sanctity. I adore you, love you and bless You in all Your divine occupations and in the marvelous effects of Your divine Childhood.

I offer You all the honor and love You received in Your holy Childhood from Your Father, Your Blessed Mother, St. Joseph, St. John the Baptist, St. Gabriel, and from the other angels and saints who are in any special way associated with Your divine Childhood.

Oh most lovable Child, I adore all Your thoughts and designs and Your most burning love for me. You were thinking of me, and loved me without interruption in Your Childhood. You cherished Your plan and Your strong desire to imprint upon my heart an image of Your divine Childhood, that is, to make me enter into a state of holy and sacred childhood, which should imitate and honor the meekness, simplicity, humility, purity of body and spirit, the obedience and innocence of Your holy Childhood.

Oh my Jesus, I give myself to You to accomplish Your plan and desire and to enter into this state. I will strive from this point on, with the help of your holy grace, which I invoke with my whole heart, to become meek, humble, simple, pure, obedient, free of all arrogance, bitterness and malice, like a child, so that I may render some small honor to Your Childhood which so deserves to be honored.

# Wednesday

## *The Hidden Life of Jesus*

Oh Jesus, You had so many and such great things to do on earth:
converting so many souls, working so many miracles, doing so much
good by Your blessed example and holy preaching if You had gone
out among men, yet You did not will to do this. Instead Your choice
on earth was a life hidden and unknown until the age of thirty,
performing in that time no outward act that might make You known
to men. You remained hidden and withdrawn into the Father,
in whom Your mind, heart, thoughts, desires and affections were
uninterruptedly enclosed. You chose this hidden life to honor Your
hidden life from all eternity in the bosom of Your Father, and to teach
us that solitude and retreat are pleasing to You.

Of the thirty-four years of Your life upon earth, no more than four
were spent in active interaction among men, while thirty were spent in
retreat and solitude.

Blessed are You, oh good Jesus, for all the glory You gave Your
Father during these thirty years of Your hidden life!

Grant that I, in their honor, may henceforth love retreat and
solitude, both interior and exterior. Draw me apart and hide me in
Yourself.

Absorb my mind into Yours, my heart into Your heart and my life
into Your life.

I desire henceforth, with the help of Your grace, to make every
effort to withdraw my thoughts and affections from all things into You,
oh my Jesus, as into my place of refuge, my center, my element and
my paradise, outside of which all else is hell and perdition.

I wish to dwell ever in You, following your commandment:

*Manete in me;*
"Abide in me" (John 15:4),

that is, in Your spirit, Your love, Your sentiments and inclinations,
never to leave You again.

Oh most great and most adorable Jesus, You willed to lead an
unknown and despised life, a life base and abject in the eyes of men, a
life of poverty, labor and suffering, bearing the name and following the

trade of carpenter, to teach us first by example what You later taught us by words, namely, that

"what is high to men is an abomination before God";
*quod hominibus altum est, abominatio est ante Deum* (Luke 16:15).

Oh Jesus, imprint this truth deeply in my mind and firmly implant in my heart a great hatred and horror of all fame, praise, greatness and vanity, and for all that catches and dazzles the eyes of men, giving me a very strong love for all that involves lowliness, abjection and humiliation.

Oh Jesus, You are God like Your Heavenly Father and You are but one God with Him; You have but one power and operation, and with Him You are the creator, preserver and governor of our vast universe.

From all eternity You and the Father emanate a God and a Divine Person, that is, the Holy Spirit, who is God even as the Father and You.

This and other exalted things worthy of Your supreme greatness, You accomplish. Yet in Your hidden and laborious life on earth, I see that You lower Yourself to the commonest and most lowly actions of human life, such as eating, drinking, sleeping, working, earning Your living with the toil of Your hands and in the sweat of Your brow.

I am filled with wonder and consolation because You are no less great and admirable in small things than in great. In these lowly commonplace activities You rendered infinitely great glory to the omnipotent Father because, oh Jesus, You performed all actions, even the smallest and most ordinary, not with common or ordinary dispositions, but with an infinite love for the Father and for us. You merited and acquired, by the power of Your holy actions, a special grace for all our acts, to enable us to perform them meritoriously.

Hence we can and must do everything in a devout manner. Otherwise we nullify and waste the graces You have acquired for us in the performance of like things. Do not allow this to happen, oh good Jesus! Give me the grace You have acquired for me by Your holy actions, so that I may perform all my own acts with holiness.

This is my desire and my resolve. Grant me grace to carry it out purely for you glory, that in the future I may offer up all my acts, even the smallest, in honor of Yours and that I may, as far as possible, perform my tasks with the dispositions and intentions that exalted the lowliness of all Your most humble, human deeds.

9

# Thursday

## *The Public Life of Christ on Earth and in the Most Blessed Sacrament*

Oh most lovable Jesus, You live, reign and commune for all eternity with the Eternal Father and the Holy Spirit. How rich is this communion and how delightful to You! What glory and praise You receive from the Father and the Holy Spirit!

Yet You willed to come forth from the bosom of the Father to appear on earth, to commune, eat and drink in familiar visible companionship, not only with Your Blessed Mother, St. Joseph and the holy apostles and disciples, but even with sinners, from who you received all kinds of outrages and indignities. You willed to do this:

- By communing with Your Blessed Mother, St. Joseph, the holy apostles and the disciples, to give homage to Your divine and holy communion with the Father and the Holy Spirit from all eternity.
- By the pain You suffered from communing with sinners, to deliver us from the punishment, so rightly deserved by our sins, of being reduced for ever to the wretched company of demons, and to make us worthy to live eternally in the company of the angels and saints, Your Blessed Mother, and the three Divine Persons.
- In order to show us how true are Your words: Your delights are to be with the children of men (Prov. 8:31).
- To acquire for us, by the merit of Your active life, the grace we need to behave virtuously in our relations with one another.
- In order that the perfection of Your holy and divine conduct in Your relations with other men might serve as a model and example of the way we should act towards our neighbor.

I adore You, oh Jesus, I bless You and love You for all these things.

I adore You in Your public life and active ministry, which lasted from Your thirtieth year to the day of Your death. I adore and give You glory for everything in this period of Your life, inward and outward, that is, all the actions, words, teachings, miracles, journeys, labors and weariness, and for all Your thoughts, feelings, intentions, affections and inner dispositions.

I bless You for all the glory You rendered to the Eternal Father.

I offer You all the love and honor accorded during the time of Your active life by all the holy souls who came in contact with You. I also offer You all my own associations and contacts, whether past or future, in homage to Your own, and I implore You to cause all my actions relating to my neighbor to be consecrated to the glory of Your public life.

Oh Jesus, I adore the thoroughly holy and divine dispositions which characterized Your activity among men. With what dignity, charity, meekness, patience, modesty, detachment from creatures and attention to God did You move and act in the world of men! Oh my Savior, I desire that such dispositions may henceforth characterize all my relations with my neighbor.

Alas! How far I am from such perfection and how many faults I have committed in the days gone by! For all these I beg Your forgiveness, imploring You to implant in me all the dispositions I have set down above.

Oh Lord, You were not satisfied with having lived and communed with mankind during Your mortal life. When You were on the point of returning to heaven, Your most insatiable love and Your exceedingly great desire to prove the tremendous truth that Your delight is to be with the children of men inspired You to devise a most admirable invention that would keep You ever with us, and give Yourself to us with all the essence of Your riches and wonders. All this was accomplished by means of the Holy Eucharist, which is a compendium of all Your wonders and the greatest of all the effects produced by Your love for us.

Oh love, oh goodness, how is it that I am not utterly transformed into love and praise for You?

Oh Jesus, forgive me my past abuse of so great a grace, grant that in the future I may make a better use of this Divine Sacrament and that, as You find Your delight in being with me, I may also find all my delight in Your company, in thinking of You, and in loving and glorifying You.

# Friday

## *The Sufferings and Death of Jesus*

O Jesus, You are the love and the delight of God and the angels, of heaven and earth. You are the God of consolation, the source of all joy and bliss; You are joy and blessedness itself.

And yet, when I behold You on the final day of Your mortal life, I see that You are the object of the wrath and persecution of heaven, earth, hell, of God, men and all creatures. I see the universe and the powers of evil in league against You, expending all their energies in making You suffer. You are, as it were, a target exposed to every volley of contradiction and outrage.

I behold You so filled with sorrow, anguish and torments in every part of Your body and soul, that You seem to be transformed into pain and sufferings. Hence, the prophet Isaiah calls You "the Man of Sorrows," *Virum dolorum* (Is. 53:3).

Oh my dearest Jesus, what has reduced You to so pitiable a state? It is Your goodness, my Savior, and the excess of Your love.

Oh my sweet love, let me adore and love and bless You in all Your sufferings, both interior and exterior; let me adore in You the holy and divine dispositions of Your suffering. With what submission to Your Father's will, with what deep humiliation under the burden of all the sins of the world, with what charity toward us, with what meekness and patience towards Your enemies You endured the magnitudes of all sufferings.

How ashamed I am to behold my Jesus suffering so extremely, with such dispositions, while I see how sensitive I am to the slightest pain, and so far from sharing His dispositions!

Oh good Jesus, I give myself to You to suffer all that You will and I offer You all that I have suffered and am yet to suffer in my whole life. May it please You to unite my works and trials with Yours; bless them through Yours; use them as Your own, to glorify the Father and to honor Your holy Passion. Grant that I may share in the love, humility and other dispositions with which You suffered.

Oh most lovable Jesus, the torments of the cross and of death were borne with so much love for the Father and for us that the Holy Spirit speaks of the day of Your passion as the day of Your Heart's joy (Songs 3:11) to show that You found joy and satisfaction in suffering.

Oh my Savior, let me also find my joy and all my happiness in this world in trials and labors, in contempt and sufferings, if by them I can give You greater glory and love! Implant these dispositions in my soul, and imprint upon my heart intense hatred for the delights and pleasures of this earth, and a particular affection for hard work and suffering.

Oh Jesus, I contemplate and adore You, agonizing and dying on the cross. I adore:

- Your last thoughts, words, actions and sufferings,
- the last use of Your bodily senses and of the faculties of Your soul,
- the last graces You infused into the soul of Your Blessed Mother and the other persons who remained at the foot of the cross;
- Your last acts of adoration and love for the Heavenly Father;
- the last sentiments and dispositions of Your Heart and soul
- and the last breath that yielded up Your life.

I offer You the last moment of my life and my death in honor of Your holy death and the consummation of Your life.

Bless my death, oh Jesus, my Savior, and sanctify it by Your own; unite it to Yours. Grant that I may share the holy and divine dispositions with which You died.

Grant, if it please You, that the last things of my life, that my last breath may be consecrated to the honor of Your last breath, and that it may be an act of most pure and perfect love for You.

13

# Saturday

## *The Life of Jesus in Mary and that of Mary in Jesus*

Oh Jesus, only Son of God, only Son of Mary, I contemplate and adore You living and reigning in Your most holy Mother, the divine Author of her existence. St. Paul says: You are all and do all in all things (Eph. 1:23; I Cor. 12:6), so surely You are and do all in Your most holy Mother.

- You are her life, her soul, her heart, her spirit, her riches.
- You are in her and, accomplishing greater works and giving to Yourself, in and by her, greater glory than in all the other creatures of heaven and earth.
- You are in her, clothing her with Your qualities and perfections, inclinations and dispositions, imprinting in her a most perfect image of Yourself, of all Your states, mysteries, and virtues, and making her so like You, that whoever sees Jesus sees Mary, and he who sees Mary beholds Jesus.

Blessed are You, O Jesus, for all that You are and all that You accomplish in Your most holy Mother!

I offer You all the delights, all the love and all the glory You ever had or ever shall have in her.

Oh Mother of Jesus, I honor and venerate your most holy and admirable life in Your Son Jesus:

- a life resplendent with every kind of virtue and perfection;
- a life of which one single moment is more dear to God than all the lives of angels and men;
- a life that gives more honor and love to God than all other lives combined in heaven and on earth.

This life is none other than the life of your Son Jesus, which He communicates to you from moment to moment by a most particular and ineffable favor.

Blessed are you, oh holy Virgin, for all the honor you have given to your Well-beloved Son in your whole life.

I offer you all my life, O Mother of life and grace, and I consecrate it all to the honor of your life, and with my whole heart I beg your Son

14

Jesus, the God of life and love, to grant by His great goodness that my whole life may pay continual and eternal homage to His most holy life and to yours.

O Jesus, God of my life and of my heart, You have a very great desire to dwell in me, and to make me live in You an entirely holy and heavenly life.

Forgive me for all the ways I have obstructed the fulfillment of Your desire by my sins and infidelities.

Eradicate the corrupt and depraved life of the old Adam in me, and in its place establish Your holy and perfect life.

Dwell in all Your fullness in my spirit, heart and soul, and there accomplish all the works You desire for Your glory.

Love Yourself in me, and in me glorify Yourself in every way that You desire.

O Mother of Jesus, if it please you, obtain from your Son the accomplishment of these things in me.

# Second Meditation for Sunday

## *Christ's Life of Glory in Heaven, after His Resurrection and Ascension*

O Jesus, I have considered and adored You in Your mortal life, in the agony of the Cross, in the shadow of death and in the chill of the Sepulcher. Let me me now adore and contemplate You in the exaltation, brightness and delights of the life of glory and blessedness You entered by Your Resurrection, which You have enjoyed in heaven in the bosom of the Father since Your Ascension.

O immortal and glorious life of my Jesus!

O life entirely free from the sorrow and suffering of this earth!

O life completely hidden and absorbed in God!

O life of nothing but love, and of love most pure. In His heavenly life, Jesus has no other thought than to love His Father, and to love us for His Father. He sought to love, bless and glorify His Father for us, to offer us to His Father and to intercede for us with Him!

O most holy life, most pure and most divine!

O life replete with unutterable joy and exultation!

O life that enjoys the fullness of glory, greatness and bliss which is God!

O my Dear Jesus, what joy for my heart to behold You living such a life!

May Your most lovable Father be blessed forever for having brought You into heaven.

O Jesus, most worthy of love, not only are You in Yourself living a life of glory and blessedness, but so also are all the angels and saints who are with You in heaven. You live in them, You communicate to them Your glorious and immortal life, You are glorious and blessed in them, as St. Paul testifies in the words: *omnia in omnibus, "You are all in all things"* (1 Cor. 12:6).

It is You who adores, praises, and loves Your Eternal Father in them and by them.

Blessed are You for all these things, O Good Jesus. I refer and offer to You the glorified and blessed life of all the citizens of heaven, together with all the love and praise they give You now and shall give You forever, in homage to the life of bliss and glory which You have in Yourself. I beg all Your angels and saints to love and glorify You for

16

me, and to associate me with all the love and glory they give You and shall give You forever.

O Jesus, object of all desire, I know that You bear me an infinite love, and by Your extreme zeal for Your glory, most ardently desire to be perfectly loved and glorified in me. You have an infinite desire to draw me to You in heaven, that You may live perfectly in me and fully establish in me the kingdom of Your glory and Your love.

You will not live and reign perfectly in me so long as I am on earth. Therefore, O my Savior, I no longer desire to live on earth except to long without ceasing after heaven.

Heaven! O heaven! How desirable are you; how you call to our love! O God of heaven, when will the time come for me to see Your holy face?

When will You live fully in me and when will I love You perfectly? O earthly life, how hard, how unbearable are you!

O God of my life and of my heart, how long and cruel is this life in which You are so little loved and so much offended! But what consoles me, Lord, is that the great apostle, St. Paul, tells me that Your Father has given us life and raised us from the dead, and caused us to sit with You and in You in heaven:

*Convivificavit nos in Christo, et conresuscitavit; et consedere fecit in coelestibus in Christo Jesu* (Eph. 2:5).

*God brought us to life in Christ, resurrected us with Him, and gave us a place in heaven with Christ Jesus.*

Hence I live with You in heaven, O Jesus, and there I share in all the love, glory and praises You give to the All-glorious Father, whether by Yourself or through the angels and saints.

Indeed, if I am united to You by grace, I can say that I am uninterruptedly loving and praising and glorifying the Eternal Father most perfectly, in You and with You, with the same love, praise and glory with which You glorify and love Him. Because I am one with You, as the member is one with the head, I can say with St. Augustine:

> Wherever my head is, I am, and I live by His life, and all that is His is mine, and I share in all that He does, all His acts and activities belong to me, and in Him and with Him I do everything that He does.

Consequently, O my dear Jesus, I am even now in heaven with Your Blessed Mother, with all Your angels and saints, and especially in company with those to whom I am particularly united. I participate in all their praise and love of You, and indeed I can say with truth that I ceaselessly love and glorify Your Father and You in them and with them. Both they and I are members of one identical Head and one identical body. We are, therefore, all one. Consequently, all that is theirs is mine. I share, therefore, all they do; indeed I do in them and with them all that they do.

What a consolation it is for me to know that I am already in heaven, and that I there love and glorify God without ceasing!

Lord Jesus, how can I possibly love You or thank You enough for having united me in so close and so holy a union with You and with all Your saints, and for having given me, by this union, such great and profitable means of praising and loving You perpetually in heaven and on earth?

O my Savior, let me praise You and love You on earth as in heaven!

May I live on earth a life in conformity with the life I lead in You and in Your saints in heaven!

May I do on earth what I do with You and with Your saints in heaven, that is, may I be ever engaged, without interruption, in loving and praising You!

May I begin my heaven in this world, seeking all my joy and satisfaction in blessing and loving You and in doing all Your holy will, in striving courageously and faithfully to complete the work of grace You desire to accomplish in me, so that once this work is finished and perfected, You may come and take me with You into the kingdom of Your eternal love, that I may there love and magnify You perfectly, without ceasing, and forever!

19

# Three Special Days of the Week

There are three week-days that should stand out above the others, and be spent with more devotion and attention to God.

Monday should be consecrated to the honor of the first day of Christ's life in the world. On this day you should renew your desire to begin a new life for Our Lord, and resolve to spend the week devotedly in His service.

Friday is dedicated to the last day of Our Lord's life on earth. You ought to regard every Friday as though it were the last day of your life, and spend it accordingly.

Saturday is consecrated to the honor of the life of Jesus in Mary and of Mary in Jesus, a life to which all Christians are bound to have special devotion. On Saturday you should render love and praise to the most Blessed Virgin with more than usual zeal and affection, and try to make reparation for having fallen away during the week from your duties to her and her Son. So, too, at the close of this day, it is well to honor the Blessed Virgin in the last day and the last hour of her life.

# ADDENDA

# A Note on the Translator

In late 1941, the young **Thomas Merton** left his existence in the world to seek the freedom of cloistered life.

At the Trappist Abbey of Our Lady of Gethsemani novices were immersed in work and silence for two years before beginning serious study. Because of his mastery of language, one assignment given to the young frater (as novices were then called) was to translate certain spiritual classics from French. During Lent of 1943, he was given *The Life and Kingdom of Jesus* by St. John Eudes with an aggressive deadline for completion. His early autobiography describes the harrowing work:

*Thomas Merton*

> "After the Conventual Mass, I would get out book and pencil and papers and go to work at one of the long tables in the novitiate scriptorium, filling the yellow sheets as fast as I could, while another novice took them and typed them as soon as they were finished."[1]

Despite this pressure from the publisher, the project was completed on time. Merton's superior called the finished product "the best translation of any of the works of St. John Eudes that he had seen."[2] Archbishop Fulton Sheen agreed in his introduction to this edition of *The Kingdom*, exulting that the spiritual treatise was "now so ably translated into English."[3]

This took place years before Merton's "Seven Storey Mountain" was released to the public, so his name did not yet hold great value to the publishers. In the spirit of humility and silence, Merton accepted for his translation to be attributed simply to "A Trappist Father in The Abbey of Our Lady of Gethsemani."[4]

1    Thomas Merton, *The Seven Storey Mountain* (New York: Harcourt, Brace & Company, 1948), 401.

2    Benjamin Clark, OCSO, "Thomas Merton's Gethsemani: Part 1, the Novitiate Years," *The Merton Annual, vol. 4* (1991): 250.

3    Fulton J Sheen, Introduction to *The Life and Kingdom of Jesus in Christian Souls,* by St. John Eudes (New York: PJ Kennedy & Sons, 1946), xix.

4    The attribution to a "Trappist *father*" is curious given that Merton would not be ordained until 1949. However, there is no doubt that the work is his. Fr. Benjamin Clark OCSO was the "other novice" referred to in the Seven Storey Mountain. Fr. Clark recalls:

> "I remember one such assignment which Merton records (SSM, p. 401). Gethsemani had entered a contract to translate the work of St. John Eudes for the publication of a new edition. Several of the monks had been assigned volumes to translate, and Merton was given The Kingdom of Jesus in Christian Souls. The publishers had allowed only a short time for the work to be completed and so I was assigned to help Merton meet the deadline. I typed the finished copy in triplicate as Merton dashed off the original on sheets of yellow paper." "Thomas Merton's Gethsemani," p. 249.

# About St. John Eudes

Born in France on November 14, 1601, St. John Eudes' life spanned the "Great Century." The Age of Discovery had revolutionized technology and exploration; the Council of Trent initiated a much-needed reform in the Church; among the common people, it was the dawn of a golden age of sanctity and mystic fervor.

## His Spiritual Heritage

No fewer than seven Doctors of the Church had lived in the previous century. Great reformers like St. Francis de Sales, St. Teresa of Avila, and St. John of the Cross had left an indelible mark on the Catholic faith. Their influence was still fresh as St. John Eudes came onto the scene.

He was educated by the Jesuits in rural Normandy. He was
ordained into the Oratory of Jesus and Mary, a society of priests
which had just been founded on the model of St. Philip Neri's
Oratory in Rome. The founder was Cardinal Pierre de Bérulle, a man
renowned for his holiness and named "the apostle of the Incarnate
Word" by Pope Urban VII. Rounding out St. John Eudes' heritage
is the influence of the Discalced Carmelites. His spiritual director,
Cardinal Bérulle himself, had brought sisters from St. Teresa of
Avila's convent to help found the Carmel in France. John Eudes would
later become spiritual director to a Carmelite convent himself. Their
cloister prayed constantly for his missionary activity.

## His Life of Ministry

As an avid participant in a wave of re-evangelization in France,
St. John Eudes' principal apostolate was preaching parish missions.
Spending anywhere from 4 to 20 weeks in each parish, he preached
over 120 missions across his lifetime, always with a team of confessors
providing the sacrament around the clock, and catechists meeting daily
with small groups of parishioners.

Early in his priesthood, an outbreak of plague hit St. John Eudes'
native region and he rushed to provide sacraments to the dying. The
risk of contagion was so great no one else dared to approach the
victims. In order to protect his Oratorian brothers from contagion,
St. John Eudes took up residence in a large empty cider barrel outside
of the city walls until the plague had ended.

## His Foundations

During his missions he heard countless confessions himself, including
those from women forced into prostitution. Realizing that they needed
intense healing and support, he began to found "Houses of Refuge" to
help them get off the street and begin a new life. In 1641 he founded
the Sisters of Our Lady of Charity of the Refuge to continue this
work. They would live with the penitent women and provide them
with constant support. Today, these sisters are known as the Good
Shepherd Sisters, inspired by their fourth vow of zeal to go out seeking
the "lost sheep."

Occasionally, St. John Eudes would return to the site of a previous
mission. To his dismay, he found that the fruits of the mission were
consistently fading for lack of support. The crucial piece in need of

25

change was the priesthood. At that time, the only way to be trained as a priest was through apprenticeship. The result of this training was so horribly inconsistent that the term "hocus pocus" was invented during this time to describe the corrupted Latin used by poorly trained priests during the consecration at mass. In 1643 he left the Oratory and founded the Congregation of Jesus and Mary to found a seminary. Seminary training was a radical brand-new concept which had just been proposed by the Council of Trent.

## His Mark on the Church

At a mission in 1648 St. John Eudes authored the first mass in history in honor of the Heart of Mary. In 1652 he built the first church under the Immaculate Heart's patronage: the chapel of his seminary in Coutances, France. During the process of his canonization, Pope St. Pius X named St. John Eudes "the father, doctor, and apostle of liturgical devotion to the hearts of Jesus and Mary." The Heart of Jesus because he created the first Feast of the Sacred Heart in 1672, just one year before St. Margaret Mary Alacoque had her first apparition of the Sacred Heart.

Although his Marian devotion was intense from a tender age, the primary inspiration for this feast came from St. John Eudes' theology of baptism. From the beginning of his missionary career he taught that Jesus continues His Incarnation in the life of each baptized Christian. As we give ourselves to Christ, our hands become His hands, our heart is transformed into His heart. Mary is the ultimate exemplar of this. She gave her heart to God so completely that she and Jesus have just one heart between them. Thus, whoever sees Mary, sees Jesus, and honoring the heart of Mary is never separate from honoring the heart of Jesus.

## Doctor of the Church?

At the time of this writing, Bishops the world over have requested that the Vatican proclaim St. John Eudes as a Doctor of the Church. This would recognize his unique contribution to our understanding of the Gospel, and his exemplary holiness of life which stands out even among saints. For more information on the progress of this cause, on his writings or spirituality, or to sign up for our e-newsletter updates, contact spirituality@eudistsusa.org.

le Blond pinxit        P. Drevet sculpsit

Le Venerable Jean Eudes Instituteur de la Congregation de Jesus et Marie
de l'Ordre de Notre-Dame de Charité et de la Societé du S. Cœur de la mere Admirable.

# About the Eudist Family

During his lifetime, St. John Eudes' missionary activity had three major areas of focus.

- For priests, he provided formation, education, and the spiritual support which is crucial for their role in God's plan of salvation.
- For prostitutes and others on the margins of society, he gave them a home and bound their wounds, like the Good Shepherd with his lost sheep.
- For the laity, he preached the dignity of their baptism and their responsibility to be the hands and feet of God, to continue the Incarnation.

In everything he did, he burned with the desire to be a living example of the love and mercy of God.

These are the "family values" which continue to inspire those who continue his work. To paraphrase St. Paul, John Eudes planted seeds, which others watered through the institutions he founded, and God gave the growth. Today, the family tree continues to bear fruit:

The *Congregation of Jesus and Mary* (CJM), also known as The Eudists, continues the effort to form and care for priests and other leaders within the Church. St. John Eudes called this the mission of "teaching the teachers, shepherding the shepherds, and enlightening those who are the light of the world." Continuing his efforts as a missionary preacher, Eudist priests and brothers "audaciously seek to open up new avenues for evangelization," through television, radio, and new media.

The *Religious of the Good Shepherd* (RGS) continue outreach to women in difficult situations, providing them with a deeply needed place of refuge and healing while they seek a new life. St. Mary Euphrasia drastically expanded the reach of this mission which now operates in over 70 countries worldwide. A true heiress of St. John Eudes, St. Mary Euphrasia exhorted her sisters: "We must go after the lost sheep with no other rest than the cross, no other consolation than work, and no other thirst than for justice."

In every seminary and House of Refuge founded by St. John Eudes, he also established a *Confraternity of the Holy Heart of Jesus and Mary* for the laity, now known as the Eudist Associates. The mission he gave them was twofold: First, "To glorify the divine Hearts of Jesus and Mary... working to make them live and reign in their own heart through diligent imitation of their virtues." Second, "To work for the salvation of souls... by practicing, according to their abilities, works of charity and mercy and by attaining numerous graces through prayer for the clergy and other apostolic laborers."

The *Little Sisters of the Poor* were an outgrowth of this confraternity. St. Jeanne Jugan was formed as a consecrated woman within the Eudist Family. She discovered the great need for love and mercy among the poor and elderly and the mission took on a life of its own. She passed on to them the Eudist intuition that the poor are not simply recipients of charity, they provide an encounter with Charity Himself: "My little ones, never forget that the poor are Our Lord... In serving the aged, it is He Himself whom you are serving."

A more recent "sprout" on the tree was founded by Mother Antonia Brenner in Tijuana, Mexico. After raising her children in Beverly Hills and suffering through divorce, she followed God's call to become a live-in prison minister at the *La Mesa* penitentiary. The *Eudist Servants of the 11th Hour* was founded so that other women in the latter part of their lives could imitate her in "being love" to those most in need.

The example St. John Eudes set for living out the Gospel has inspired many more individuals and organizations throughout the world. For more information about the Eudist family, news on upcoming publications, or for ways to share in our mission, contact us at spirituality@eudistsusa.org.

# A Holy Week Every Week: Weekday Meditations

These are excerpts from *The Life and the Kingdom of Jesus: A Treatise on Christian Perfection for Use by Clergy or Laity,* translated from French by Thomas Merton in The Abbey of Our Lady of Gethsémani and published by Kennedy & Sons in New York, 1946.

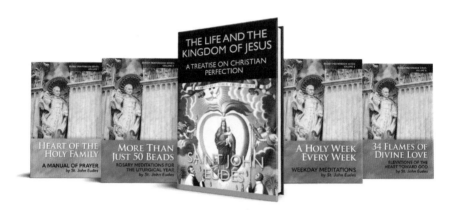

*The Life and the Kingdom of Jesus* as well as other titles in this series, *Heart of the Holy Family, More Thank Just 50 Beads* and *34 Flames of Divine Love* by St. John Eudes can be found in the Eudist bookstore on amazon.com.

# More by Eudist Press

- *A Heart on Fire: St. John Eudes, a Model for the New Evangelization*
- *Spiritual Itinerary for Today with St. John Eudes*
- *Eudist Lectionary: A St. John Eudes Reader*

## Eudist Prayerbook Series

- Volume 1: *Heart of the Holy Family:*
  *A Manual of Prayer*
- Volume 2: *More than Just 50 Beads:*
  *Rosary Meditations for the Liturgical Year*
- Volume 3: *A Holy Week Every Week:*
  *Weekday Meditations*
- Volume 4: *34 Flames of Divine Love:*
  *Elevations of the Heart Towards God*

## Biography

- *St. John Eudes: Worker for the New Evangelization in the 17th Century*
- *In All Things, the Will of God: St. John Eudes Through His Letters*

# More by St. John Eudes

## St. John Eudes' Selected Works

- *The Life and Kingdom of Jesus in Christian Souls*
- *The Sacred Heart of Jesus*
- *The Admirable Heart of Mary*
- *The Priest: His Dignity and Obligations*
- *Meditations*
- *Letters and Shorter Works*

## Other Works

- *Man's Contract with God in Holy Baptism*
- *The Wondrous Childhood of the Mother of God*

Made in the USA
Columbia, SC
08 July 2018